WEREWOLVES

monster Chronicles

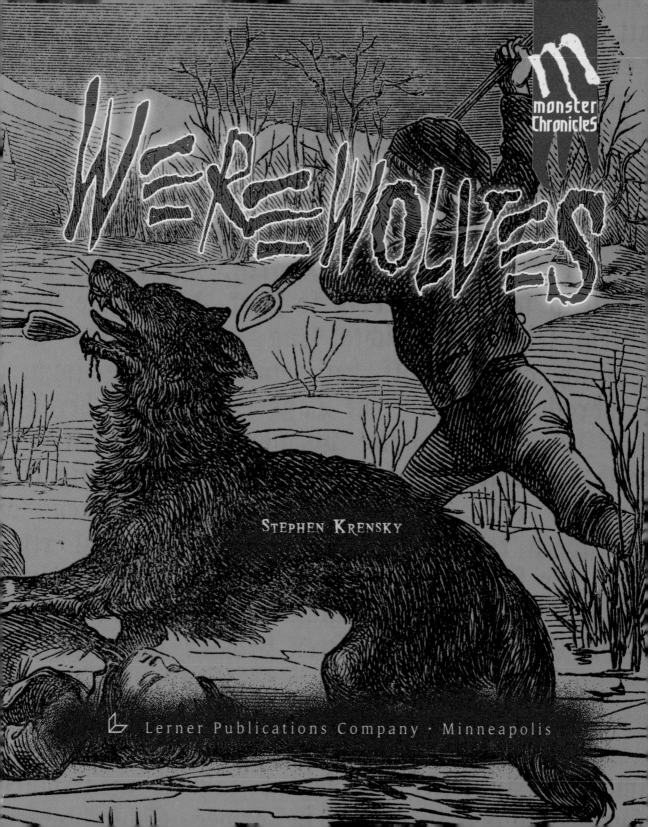

WEREWOLVES

Stephen Krensky

Lerner Publications Company · Minneapolis

Monster Chronicles

Lerner Publications Company
A division of Lerner Publishing Group
241 First Avenue North
Minneapolis, MN 55401 U.S.A.

Website address: www.lernerbooks.com

Library of Congress Cataloging-in-Publication Data

Krensky, Stephen.
    Werewolves / by Stephen Krensky.
        p. cm. — (Monster chronicles)
    Includes bibliographical references and index.
    ISBN-13: 978-0-8225-5922-1 (lib. bdg. : alk. paper)
    ISBN-10: 0-8225-5922-6 (lib. bdg. : alk. paper)
    1. Werewolves—Juvenile literature. 2. Werewolves in literature—Juvenile literature. 3. Werewolf films—Juvenile literature. I. Title. II. Series.
    GR830.W4K74 2007
    398'.45—dc22   2005030254

Manufactured in the United States of America
1 2 3 4 5 6 - JR - 12 11 10 09 08 07

1 PLENTY TO GROWL ABOUT

It's not easy being a werewolf. Werewolves have a lot to deal with. For starters, there are the usual issues—

TABLE OF CONTENTS

hairy palms, endless howling, and shedding too much fur on the carpet.

But those aren't the only issues. Werewolves actually have a much bigger problem. Simply put, they don't get much respect. When it comes to getting attention, vampires and ghosts hog the glory. And we're not just talking quantity. There's a quality problem too. Vampires can be charming. Ghosts are romantic or tragic. Both can be attractive, even when they're evil. Werewolves, on the other hand, are rarely shown as being attractive.

How did this lack of respect for werewolves develop? Well, even though werewolves are well known, they don't get the publicity that other creatures enjoy. When you think of vampires, you think of Dracula. And every old town has a haunted house or castle keeping ghosts in the public eye. But when you think of werewolves prowling through the night, you think of . . . That's the trouble. There are no famous werewolves—not really. And no werewolf romances or tragedies exist to make them sympathetic, either.

Werewolves have been around for thousands of years. Actually, that's part of the problem. The relationship between wolves and people goes back at least 140,000 years. Dogs, which are closely related to wolves, also began to evolve many thousands of years ago. Over time, dogs became valued companions to humans. Dogs saw the benefits of being a human's best friend. They could sit around warm campfires and be fed scraps of meat they hadn't had to hunt for.

Wolves did not see these advantages. They were known for their strength, cruelty, and fierceness. They are great and tireless hunters.

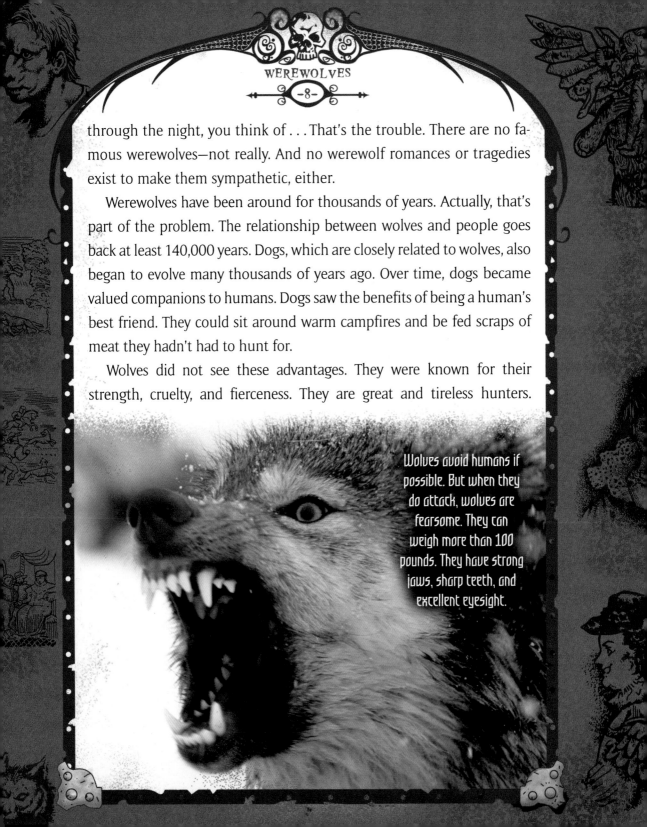

Wolves avoid humans if possible. But when they do attack, wolves are fearsome. They can weigh more than 100 pounds. They have strong jaws, sharp teeth, and excellent eyesight.

In the folktale *Little Red Riding Hood*, a wolf tries to trick a little girl by disguising itself as her grandmother. But Red Riding Hood has her doubts about "Grandma's" large paws and sharp teeth.

Traveling by day or night, they work alone or in packs—whichever will get them their prey. And this prey is never a vegetable such as spinach or broccoli. Wolves like meat, and they're not too fussy about what kind of meat. Everything from a cow to a mouse is fair game.

None of this makes a wolf very lovable. It also doesn't help to be the bad guy in bedtime stories such as *Little Red Riding Hood* and *The Three Little Pigs*. Wolves that disguise themselves as grandmothers or huff and puff to blow down houses don't make new friends easily. And beware of a "wolf in sheep's clothing"—a warning that some nasty people pretend to be nice—are words of wisdom that go all the way back to the Bible.

Still, wolves get the occasional good press. In Roman mythology, a she-wolf fed and cared for the twin babies Romulus and Remus. Romulus grew up to start the Roman Empire. A wolf also felt sorry for Mowgli, the baby in Rudyard Kipling's *The Jungle Book.* She kept him safe until he was old enough to fend for himself.

The name *wolf* was also one that many ancient warriors wore proudly. (They wore wolf skins, too, at least in cold weather.) The most famous of these warriors, Beowulf, is the hero of an Old English epic poem recorded in about A.D. 1000. (Beowulf defeats a monster named Grendel to become king, but later dies fighting a dragon. It was not easy being an Old English king.)

In Roman mythology, Romulus and Remus were abandoned as babies by an evil king. The twins were rescued by a river god and taken care of by a she-wolf.

STARTING OFF ON THE RIGHT FOOT

Of course, a regular ordinary wolf is not a werewolf. To be a werewolf, you start out as a person—and then get transformed, or changed. In fact, the word *werewolf* actually explains a lot about the beasts. *Wer* was an Old English word meaning "man." And *wolf*, of course, means "wolf." A werewolf is a man-wolf. But there are other wer beasts too. Legends from around the world feature werefoxes, wereleopards, even were-snakes. The most famous combo is probably the Egyptian sphinx, a giant statue depicting a lion body with the head of a man.

Wer animals are always on the strong and scary side. There are no *weresheep*. There are no *wereponies*. Whatever else these might be, wer animals are not cute.

A little northwest of the sphinx, King Nebuchadnezzar ruled Babylonia (part of modern-day Iraq) in the 500s B.C. Nebuchadnezzar was a powerful conqueror, but stories were whispered about him behind his back. Some people thought he was mad. Others were convinced that he spent time as a werewolf. As king, Nebuchadnezzar didn't have to worry about rumors, but they didn't help his reputation.

Many of the Egyptian gods have animal heads on human bodies. One of the most powerful is Anubis, the jackal-headed god of the underworld.

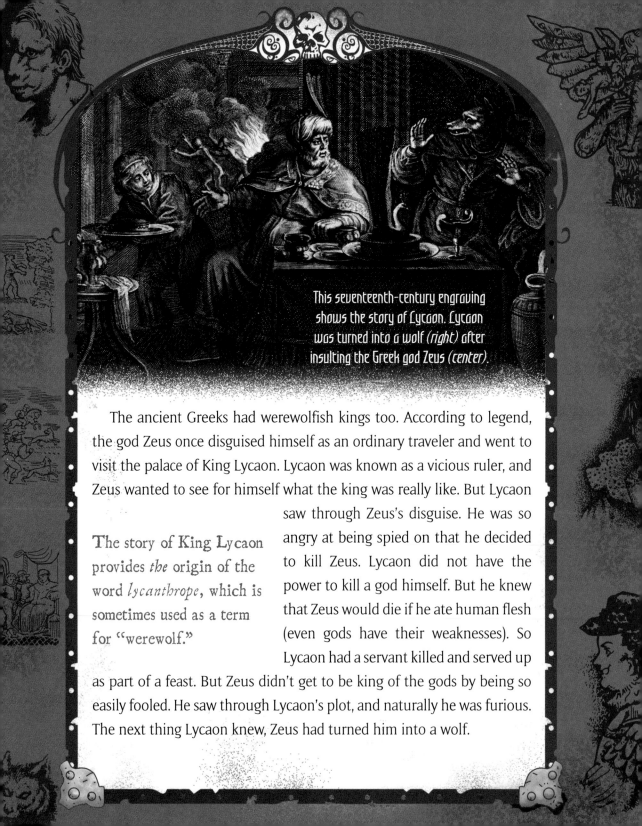

This seventeenth-century engraving shows the story of Lycaon. Lycaon was turned into a wolf *(right)* after insulting the Greek god Zeus *(center)*.

The ancient Greeks had werewolfish kings too. According to legend, the god Zeus once disguised himself as an ordinary traveler and went to visit the palace of King Lycaon. Lycaon was known as a vicious ruler, and Zeus wanted to see for himself what the king was really like. But Lycaon saw through Zeus's disguise. He was so angry at being spied on that he decided to kill Zeus. Lycaon did not have the power to kill a god himself. But he knew that Zeus would die if he ate human flesh (even gods have their weaknesses). So Lycaon had a servant killed and served up as part of a feast. But Zeus didn't get to be king of the gods by being so easily fooled. He saw through Lycaon's plot, and naturally he was furious. The next thing Lycaon knew, Zeus had turned him into a wolf.

The story of King Lycaon provides *the* origin of the word *lycanthrope*, which is sometimes used as a term for "werewolf."

The English monk known as the Venerable Bede describes wer animals in a book about the history of England, which he wrote around A.D. 731.

Other legends about werewolves were popular in places where wolves were greatly feared. In the Middle Ages (from about A.D. 500 to 1500), dark places such as the Black Forest of Bavaria, in modern-day Germany, were filled with wolves. They often attacked people who wandered across their paths. The wolves seemed so smart that frightened peasants began to think that some man-wolves must be mixed in among the packs. And so terrifying stories soon followed.

These days, dark forests are harder to find, making it more difficult for wolves or werewolves to hide out. Still, we should stay on our toes. If there's one thing werewolves do well, it's survive.

Wolves were so feared in Ireland that a special kind of dog, the Irish wolfhound, was bred to hunt them.

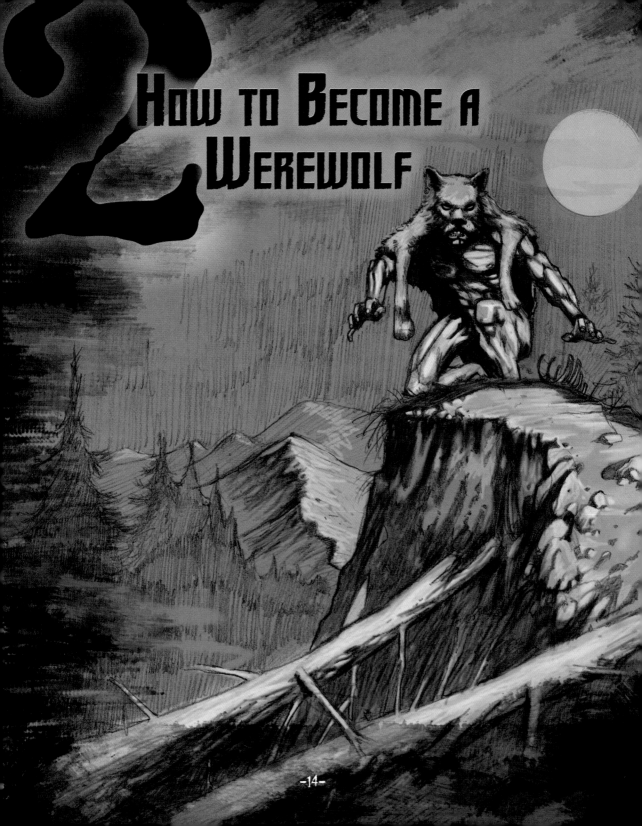

2 How to Become a Werewolf

In general, there are two kinds of werewolves. Some people deliberately set out to become werewolves. And some people become one by luck (usually bad luck).

The ones who choose the werewolf's life usually perform a traditional ritual. Becoming a werewolf is like following a recipe. Certain steps and ingredients are used in the proper order. These instructions are very precise. They involve covering your body with various ointments (none of which smell good). Or you can try the shortcut of covering yourself with a wolf hide and praying to the devil. Either approach has to be done at a specific time—usually at night and often by the light of a full moon. To finish the transformation, the person recites special words or a spell. Of course, these words must be completed before the

Some of the ointments people used to turn themselves into werewolves may have had druglike effects. The effects convinced these people that they had been transformed into werewolves.

change takes place. Once the transformation occurs, the werewolf often loses the power of speech.

For other people, becoming a werewolf is as simple (and painful) as being bitten by a werewolf. The victim doesn't die from the bite. And at first, that person would feel lucky to have survived. But soon he would notice some small changes. Wolflike urges might creep up on him over days or weeks. And by the time of the next full moon, he'd be out howling at it.

Whatever the reason for the transformation, the mythic process was similar for all. As a person actually became a werewolf, his whole

A werewolf attacks a man outside a German village in this fifteenth-century woodcut print.

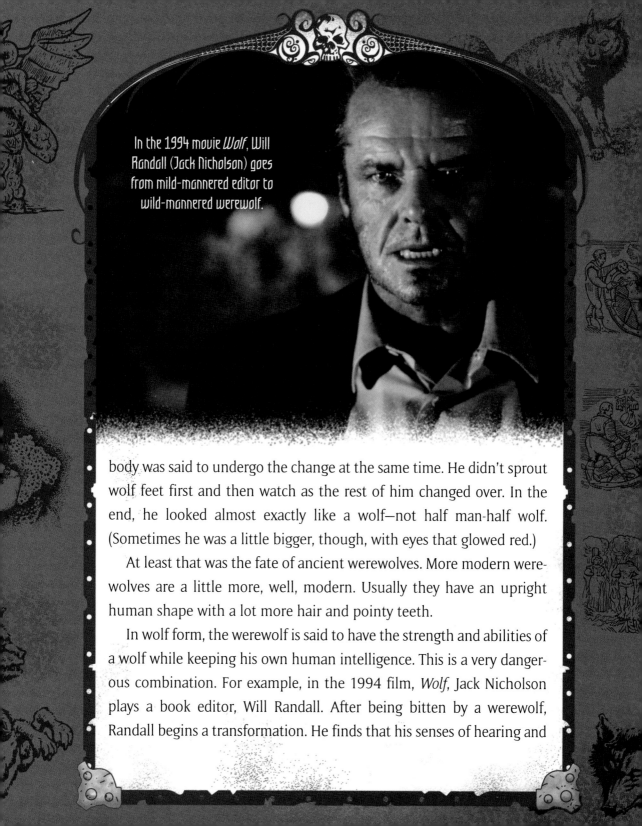

In the 1994 movie *Wolf*, Will Randall (Jack Nicholson) goes from mild-mannered editor to wild-mannered werewolf.

body was said to undergo the change at the same time. He didn't sprout wolf feet first and then watch as the rest of him changed over. In the end, he looked almost exactly like a wolf—not half man-half wolf. (Sometimes he was a little bigger, though, with eyes that glowed red.)

At least that was the fate of ancient werewolves. More modern werewolves are a little more, well, modern. Usually they have an upright human shape with a lot more hair and pointy teeth.

In wolf form, the werewolf is said to have the strength and abilities of a wolf while keeping his own human intelligence. This is a very dangerous combination. For example, in the 1994 film, *Wolf*, Jack Nicholson plays a book editor, Will Randall. After being bitten by a werewolf, Randall begins a transformation. He finds that his senses of hearing and

smell are much more powerful. He can tell when people are lying to him because he can sense fear more easily than humans can. He hears their hearts beat faster, and he smells their sweat. (Randall likes this power at first. The problems that come with it only show up later.)

DEALING WITH WEREWOLVES

In theory, a werewolf can be noble and kind. There are no laws against it. No werewolf, though, seems to turn out that way. In fact, werewolves are known for being cruel and heartless. Most of all, they are known for being hungry. And so people tried to hunt down and kill werewolves.

But this is no easy task. Sneaking up on a wolf is pretty much impossible. Wolves can smell you a mile away. Besides, catching a werewolf by surprise might not help. Swords cannot penetrate their skin. Lead bullets are said to bounce off as well. And if you were only finding this out while battling a werewolf, you'd be in big trouble. The werewolf would not be politely standing around while you poked or prodded. Most likely, he would be tearing you to shreds.

In an Armenian tradition, a sinful woman might have to take the form of a wolf for seven years as punishment. In Russia, if a mother gives birth to six girls, her seventh child will be a boy and a werewolf.

Werewolves do have their weaknesses, though. The scent of garlic and wolfsbane (an herb) repels them. They don't like five-sided objects called pentagons. But their biggest weakness is a weapon made of silver. Of these, silver bullets seem to work best.

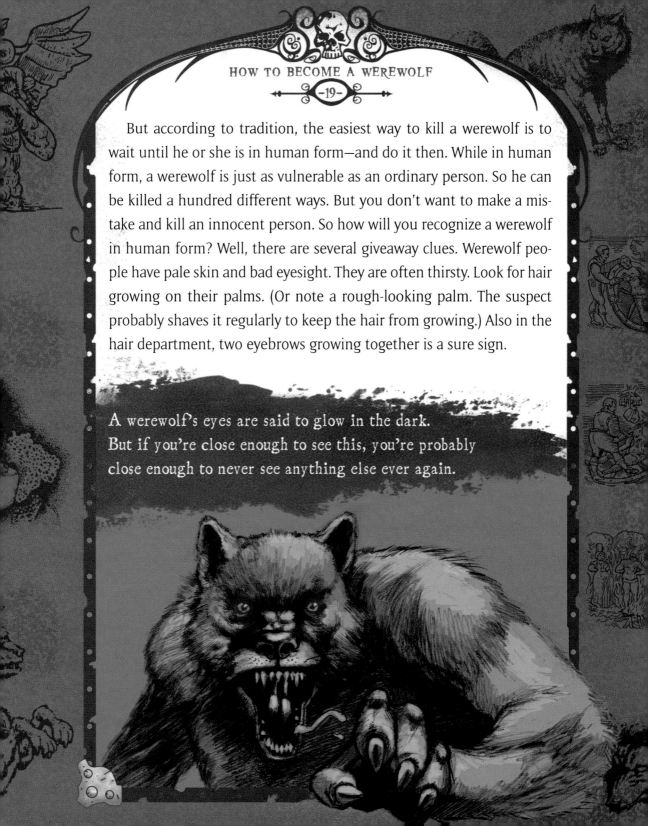

But according to tradition, the easiest way to kill a werewolf is to wait until he or she is in human form—and do it then. While in human form, a werewolf is just as vulnerable as an ordinary person. So he can be killed a hundred different ways. But you don't want to make a mistake and kill an innocent person. So how will you recognize a werewolf in human form? Well, there are several giveaway clues. Werewolf people have pale skin and bad eyesight. They are often thirsty. Look for hair growing on their palms. (Or note a rough-looking palm. The suspect probably shaves it regularly to keep the hair from growing.) Also in the hair department, two eyebrows growing together is a sure sign.

A werewolf's eyes are said to glow in the dark. But if you're close enough to see this, you're probably close enough to never see anything else ever again.

Even if they can keep their identities a secret, a lot of werewolves look for a way out of their curse. In many tales, they wish to return to their human state permanently. Being hunted down by angry villagers only makes them want it a little more. Whether it is possible for werewolves to become human again depends on how they were transformed in the first place. If they simply put on the required wolf skin (or someone else forced it on them), then taking it off again might do the trick. Rolling around in a stream or river might also help. Running water is known to ruin magic spells. Other ways include being saluted with a cross or being called three times by your baptized name.

Villagers hunt a werewolf in this illustration from a nineteenth-century French storybook.

Some traditions state that a werewolf can only be changed back to a human form permanently if it has never tasted human blood. Considering how werewolves spend their time, this has to be discouraging.

There is no surefire cure, though, and every situation is different. Meanwhile, werewolves go back and forth to human form. Some of their transformations are tied to the phases of the moon. Other werewolves can change at will. But none of them are ever free. No doubt, a lot of werewolves get pretty frustrated trying to break their curse. And that, at least, partly explains why they spend so much time howling in the night.

3 MEDIEVAL WEREWOLVES IN REAL LIFE

Countless legends exist about mythical people or creatures. These legends become more believable when supported by some evidence from the real world. Of course, what is meant by "evidence"

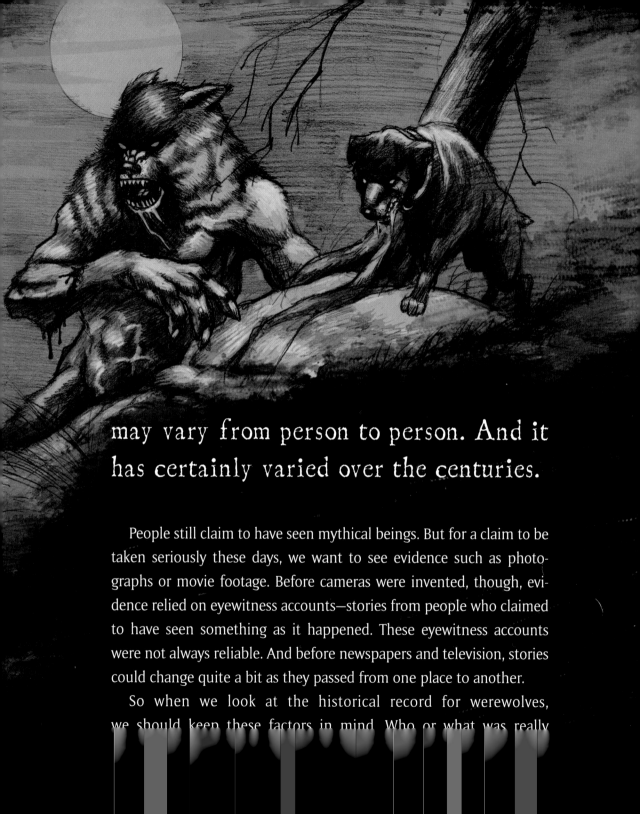

may vary from person to person. And it has certainly varied over the centuries.

People still claim to have seen mythical beings. But for a claim to be taken seriously these days, we want to see evidence such as photographs or movie footage. Before cameras were invented, though, evidence relied on eyewitness accounts—stories from people who claimed to have seen something as it happened. These eyewitness accounts were not always reliable. And before newspapers and television, stories could change quite a bit as they passed from one place to another.

So when we look at the historical record for werewolves, we should keep these factors in mind. Who or what was really

responsible for reported werewolf attacks in the past? Were they simply the acts of ordinary wolves? Or bandits wearing wolf skins to look more frightening?

WEREWOLVES OF EUROPE

History has passed down some stories of famous werewolves caught in the act. Consider the case of Gilles Garnier, a French peasant who lived in the 1500s. More than fifty local people swore they saw Garnier roaming about as a werewolf under a full moon. And Garnier wasn't just stretching his legs (whether two or four). He was going about killing children, which his neighbors naturally objected to.

France seems to have had more werewolf sightings during the 1500s than anyplace else.

Garnier was soon caught and reportedly confessed to his crimes. Once they had his confession, the authorities quickly put him to death on January 18, 1573.

A few years later, near the German city of Cologne, a similar tale arose. The countryside around Cologne is beautiful. But in those days, it was also very dangerous. Attacks from wolves were so common that only the very brave or the very foolish went out after dark.

One day a few peasants and some dogs cornered a wandering wolf in a country village. At least they thought it was a wolf. The animal darted back and forth, snarling and snapping its teeth. The peasants could not get a clear look at the beast. But then the wolf suddenly stopped moving. Witnesses claimed that he then stood up on two legs—and turned into a man. Even more amazing, this man was no stranger. He was Peter Stubbe, who lived in the village.

Stubbe was taken prisoner at once. His crime was not simply that he could turn into a wolf. (In those days, that would have been bad enough.) He also confessed to having killed a great many people while in wolf form. And he hadn't killed them nicely—he had torn them apart with his teeth and claws.

The villagers could not think of a punishment that truly fit Stubbe's brutality. But that didn't keep them from trying. He was tortured in various ways, and then he was beheaded. Afterward, the villagers burned his

German villager Peter Stubbe was accused of being a werewolf in 1589. This 1590 woodcut print shows his story.

Historical records state that many werewolves confessed to their crimes. But in the past, authorities often used brutal torture to force confessions. The accused likely would have admitted almost anything to make the pain stop.

body. The villagers believed that his mistress and daughter had helped Stubbe in his crimes, so they were also put to death.

You might think that Peter Stubbe's punishment would discourage other people from pursuing werewolf careers. But it didn't. Or at least, so said their accusers. Tens of thousands of people in Europe were accused of being werewolves during the 1500s alone.

Werewolf rumors in France lasted well into the eighteenth century. The Beast of Gevaudan (below), for example, supposedly killed more than one hundred people in central France in the 1760s.

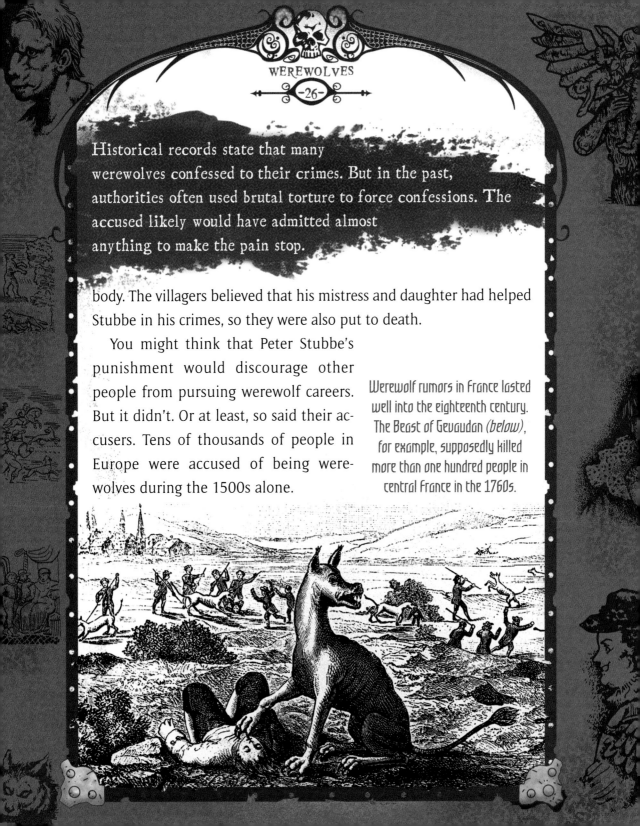

WEREWOLVES IN AMERICA

Tales of werewolves are less common in the United States, but they are not unknown. For example, there is a tale of an old man who lived in Northumberland County, Pennsylvania, around 1899. If he had just kept to himself, his neighbors might have paid less attention. But the man seemed to like a twelve-year-old girl who watched over her family's flock of sheep. Wolves were a problem in the area, but strangely, they never troubled the young girl's flock. The locals couldn't help wondering why. Maybe the old man was more than he appeared to be. Maybe he was using his influence to keep the wolves away.

Porphyria, a disease that causes an extreme sensitivity to light and changes in skin color and general appearance, has been blamed for accusations against people thought to be werewolves and vampires.

Then one night, a hunter spotted an old wolf by the light of a full moon. He fired at him—and heard the wolf yelp in pain. The wolf dodged into some thick bushes. The hunter decided it wasn't safe to follow a wounded animal at night, so he came back in the morning. Looking into the bushes where the wolf had gone, the hunter found the dead body of the old man. For the hunter and everyone else, this proved that the old man had been a werewolf. (Apparently, nobody remembered that werewolves could only be killed with *silver* bullets. They didn't consider the possibility that the hunter had simply shot an innocent man by mistake.)

No doubt some accused werewolves were completely innocent. They were unluckily caught in the wrong place at the wrong time.

Others may not have been true werewolves but may have used the fear of werewolves to cover their crimes. Some people, too, actually think they are werewolves when they aren't. Eating certain kinds of foods (containing harmful drugs) can lead these people to imagine their own

This German woodcut print made by Lucas Cranach the Elder in 1512 shows a man transforming into a werewolf. He moves like a four-legged animal attacking humans.

transformations. People suffering from certain diseases may also exhibit symptoms of werewolflike behavior. (Rabies, for example, can lead to foaming at the mouth. And if the victim happens to be big and hairy, a frightened onlooker might easily jump to the wrong conclusion.)

Lycanthropy was originally a term used to describe the process of becoming a werewolf. In modern times, the word refers to a mental illness. People who have the illness believe they have been transformed into a werewolf. Some of these patients can be treated with medications that lessen the effects of lycanthropy.

Tales of werewolves come mostly from the distant past, but there have been enough of them to put werewolves in the public eye. Once firmly established, the werewolves have shown themselves to be very unwilling to go away.

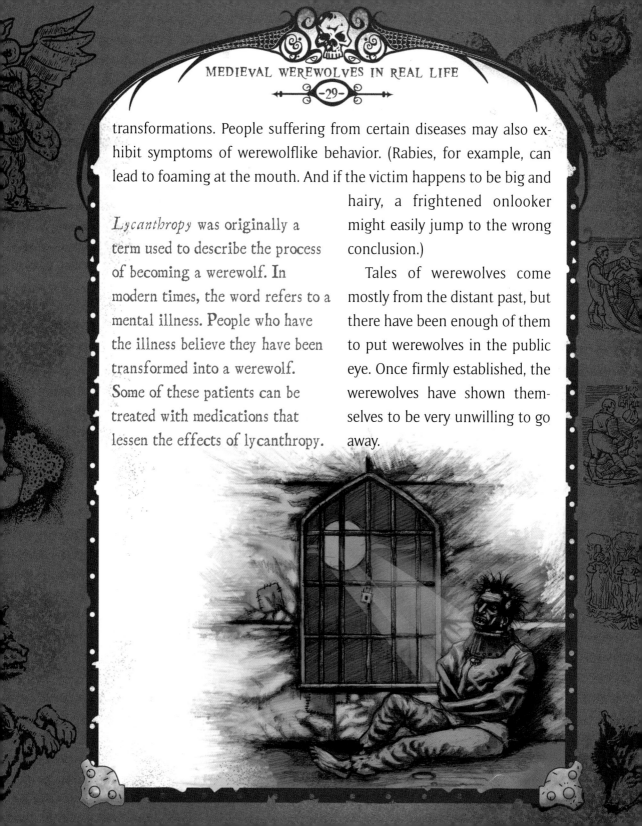

1 WEREWOLVES TURN THE PAGE

Werewolves gained a new respectability once the creature became part of literature and entertainment. The feeling of being caught between two worlds—and comfortable in neither—was something many people understood.

They had these feelings even if they
didn't like to howl at the moon or grow
hair on their palms.

Among the most famous stories of a man turning into an animal is
Beauty and the Beast. The most popular early version was published in
France in 1756. In this unusual story, a young woman is thrown into
the company of a beast-man who lives in a palace. The woman agrees
to give up her freedom and live in the palace to save her father's life.
She and the beast must learn to trust each other. But the story isn't unusual for these reasons. It's unusual because the beast gets to have a
happy ending. (Most often in such stories, the happy ending comes

In the 1931 movie version of *Dr. Jekyll and Mr. Hyde*, Fredric March (*right*) played Mr. Hyde. Hyde was a modern version of a werewolf— a normal human who transforms into a violent beast.

with a beast's death.) Of course, it helps that the beast turns into a handsome prince at the end.

The beast was not so fortunate in Robert Louis Stevenson's 1886 novel *The Strange Case of Dr. Jekyll and Mr. Hyde*. This story was inspired by the real-life William Brodie, an eighteenth-century Scottish business-man and town leader. Respectable by day, Brodie was a gambler and thief after dark. He was finally caught, sentenced to death, and hanged in 1788. Brodie was a man whose good and evil seem distinctly sepa-rated, like night and day.

In Stevenson's book, Henry Jekyll, a serious and respectable doctor, takes this idea one step further. With the aid of a special potion, Jekyll transforms himself into another person, Edward Hyde. Cruel and vio-lent, the wolfish Mr. Hyde is the opposite of Dr. Jekyll. Jekyll's goal of understanding the two sides of human nature—good and evil—may be noble. But the results are tragic.

Almost a hundred years later, horror master Stephen King wrote *Cycle of the Werewolf* (1983). The novel brings us a year in a life of a small town with big werewolf problems. The biggest is that every month another town resident dies. Joan Aiken's children's book *The Wolves of Willoughby Chase* features regular wolves. But Aiken also wrote *Midwinter Nightingale*, which includes an ambitious werewolf. In this case, he's an evil baron who's plotting to make his son the king of England. If he succeeds, the monarchy will clearly be heading in a new direction.

MOVIES WORK THEIR MAGIC

The magic of movies made werewolf transformations even more dramatic. In fact, many werewolf traditions that we think are ancient legends actually started with werewolf movies. A good example is the first full-length werewolf movie, *The Werewolf of London*, made in 1935. Here, the werewolf did not transform

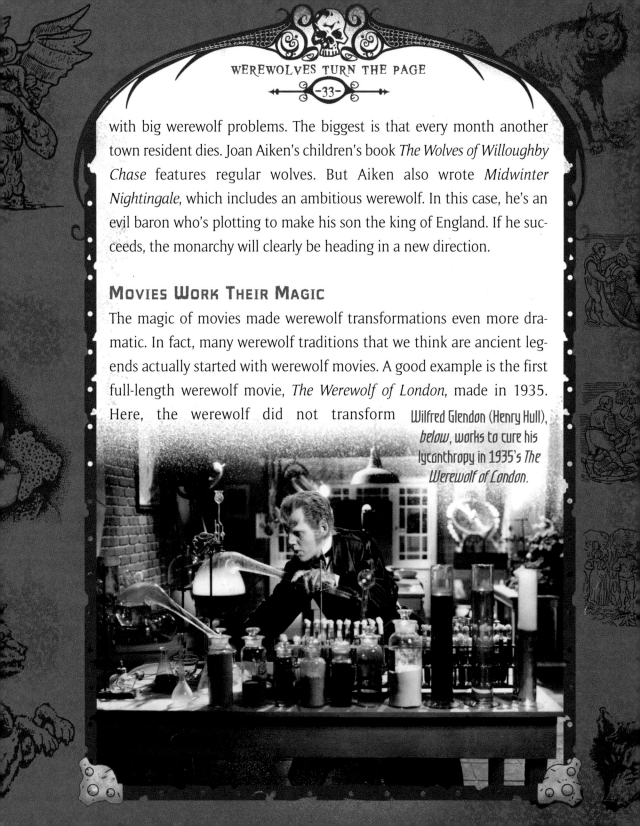

Wilfred Glendon (Henry Hull), *below*, works to cure his lycanthropy in 1935's *The Werewolf of London*.

completely into a wolf, as in old tales. Instead, he was transformed into a half man and half wolf. The reason for this didn't involve deep thoughts about the nature of the werewolf. Basically, the special effects of the time were limited. An actor dressed up as a two-legged wolf man was much easier to film.

Soon more movies appeared. *The Wolf Man* (1941) starred Lon Chaney Jr. as Larry Talbot. Talbot returns home to Europe from the United States just in time to be bitten by a gypsy. This is no ordinary nip. The bite turns him into a wolf man.

Lon Chaney Jr. *(left)* and Evelyn Ankers star in a scene from *The Wolf Man* (1941).

Several pieces of werewolf lore first appeared in this film. Among them is the idea that werewolves change from man to beast during the full moon and that they are best killed with a weapon made of silver.

In *Frankenstein Meets the Wolf Man* (1943), the two legendary monsters meet for the first time. The Wolf Man frees Frankenstein from a block of ice where he's been frozen for years. But that doesn't mean the two spend the movie getting along. Two heads, furry or otherwise, do not seem to have been better than one. Both creatures appear to be destroyed in a flood caused by the destruction of a village dam.

A 1946 movie poster from *La Belle et la Bête* (*Beauty and the Beast*). The popular film retold an old French fairy tale of a cursed prince. The prince is condemned to live as a wolflike beast until he is saved by a young woman.

In the 1950s, movies about high school kids running wild and causing trouble were popular. Actor Michael Landon took that notion a step further in *I Was a Teenage Werewolf* (1957).

In the 1950s, movies featuring troubled teenagers were popular. Among them was *I Was a Teenage Werewolf* (1957). Michael Landon played Tony Rivers, a teenager with a short temper who gets into fights. He goes to see a doctor who is supposed to help him control his temper. But the doctor is up to no good. He experiments on Tony, giving him injections that turn him into a werewolf. Sadly, Tony's violence results in the murder of other teenagers. In the end, he kills the doctor and his assistant, destroying all evidence of their

Michael Landon later starred in three long-running television series. He played Little Joe Cartwright on *Bonanza*, Charles Ingalls on *Little House on the Prairie*, and the angel Jonathan on *Highway to Heaven*.

work. The teenaged werewolf is then gunned down in a hail of police bullets. In death, he reverts to his human form, but it's a little late to get help then.

In his 1978 song "Werewolves of London," Warren Zevon (*below*) sings about a well-dressed werewolf with "perfect" hair, who sips cocktails and eats Chinese food. But good taste doesn't stop the werewolf from terrorizing the people of London.

In the 1985 movie *Teen Wolf*, Scott Howard (Michael J. Fox) gains new popularity when he transforms into a hairy beast.

Wrestling with the usual adolescent problems (girlfriends, popularity, and pimples) is the theme of the movie *Teen Wolf* (1985). Michael J. Fox stars as Scott Howard, a struggling basketball player who isn't cool and can't get a special girl to notice him. But then puberty kicks in. The next thing you know, Scott has become a werewolf. Surprisingly (and luckily for Scott), the other kids are not terrified by his makeover. In fact, they are impressed with Scott's new

In *Teen Wolf Too* (1987), Jason Bateman took over the teenage werewolf role as Scott Howard's cousin, Todd. Todd is starting college, but there are a few personal details he left off the application.

abilities. But even though Scott begins to gain the popularity he thought he always wanted, he finds himself wishing for his old life.

WEREWOLVES MOVE INTO NEW TERRITORY

Just because werewolves are usually rough and tough doesn't mean that they have no sense of humor. The 1960s television comedy series *The Munsters* featured a young werewolf named Eddie. It's safe to say that Eddie is the only werewolf in history to have a vampire mother and a Frankenstein monster father. Like *The Munsters*, Daniel Pinkwater's book, *I Was a Second Grade Werewolf*, features a school-age version of the monster. In this case, the boy delights in his newly

In the 1960s television series *The Munsters*, Butch Patrick played a young werewolf named Eddie.

acquired werewolf nature. He is frustrated, though, because he can't seem to get anyone else to notice.

In recent years, some television werewolves who were not always evil have appeared. Quentin Collins, the werewolf on the 1960s supernatural soap opera *Dark Shadows*, even had his heroic moments. And on *Buffy the Vampire Slayer*, the laid-back teenager Oz was revealed to be a werewolf. Oz's transformation is so complete that he loses his

An American Werewolf in London (1981) used groundbreaking makeup to create the werewolf David *(below)*. The film's makeup artist, Rick Baker, won an Academy Award—the first ever given to a special effects artist.

R. L. Stine's Goosebumps series of the early 1990s featured *The Werewolf of Fever Swamp* and *I Want to Be a Werewolf for Halloween.*

awareness of his human self. So he must be locked up for his (and everyone else's) own good until he changes back.

However, if werewolves really want to change their public image, they still have a long way to go. The biggest hurdle they face is finding a new way to spend their time. With only a few exceptions, all werewolves do is attack people—either to eat them or just because they can. No one expects a werewolf to find a cure for cancer or to rescue people from burning buildings. But they could improve their standing in the community with a little effort. So the next move is up to them. Until they make it, they're going to have to keep howling in the dark and dodging those silver bullets as best they can.

A werewolf, Remus J. Lupin, is featured in the fantasy novel *Harry Potter and the Prisoner of Azkaban.* Lupin is a professor at Hogwarts Academy. He keeps his transformations under control by taking a potion made of wolfsbane.

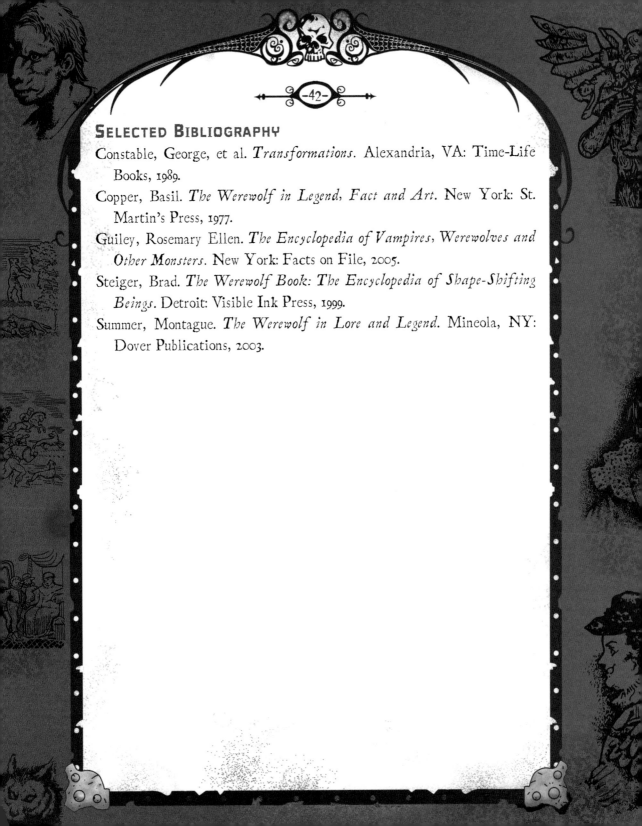

SELECTED BIBLIOGRAPHY

Constable, George, et al. *Transformations*. Alexandria, VA: Time-Life Books, 1989.

Copper, Basil. *The Werewolf in Legend, Fact and Art*. New York: St. Martin's Press, 1977.

Guiley, Rosemary Ellen. *The Encyclopedia of Vampires, Werewolves and Other Monsters*. New York: Facts on File, 2005.

Steiger, Brad. *The Werewolf Book: The Encyclopedia of Shape-Shifting Beings*. Detroit: Visible Ink Press, 1999.

Summer, Montague. *The Werewolf in Lore and Legend*. Mineola, NY: Dover Publications, 2003.

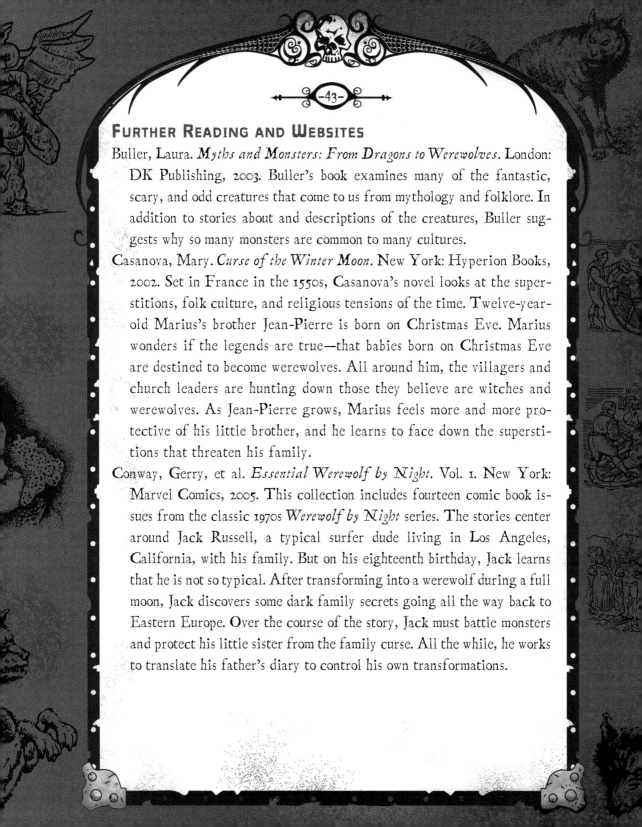

FURTHER READING AND WEBSITES

Buller, Laura. *Myths and Monsters: From Dragons to Werewolves*. London: DK Publishing, 2003. Buller's book examines many of the fantastic, scary, and odd creatures that come to us from mythology and folklore. In addition to stories about and descriptions of the creatures, Buller suggests why so many monsters are common to many cultures.

Casanova, Mary. *Curse of the Winter Moon*. New York: Hyperion Books, 2002. Set in France in the 1550s, Casanova's novel looks at the superstitions, folk culture, and religious tensions of the time. Twelve-year-old Marius's brother Jean-Pierre is born on Christmas Eve. Marius wonders if the legends are true—that babies born on Christmas Eve are destined to become werewolves. All around him, the villagers and church leaders are hunting down those they believe are witches and werewolves. As Jean-Pierre grows, Marius feels more and more protective of his little brother, and he learns to face down the superstitions that threaten his family.

Conway, Gerry, et al. *Essential Werewolf by Night*. Vol. 1. New York: Marvel Comics, 2005. This collection includes fourteen comic book issues from the classic 1970s *Werewolf by Night* series. The stories center around Jack Russell, a typical surfer dude living in Los Angeles, California, with his family. But on his eighteenth birthday, Jack learns that he is not so typical. After transforming into a werewolf during a full moon, Jack discovers some dark family secrets going all the way back to Eastern Europe. Over the course of the story, Jack must battle monsters and protect his little sister from the family curse. All the while, he works to translate his father's diary to control his own transformations.

Garmon, Larry Mike. *Blood Moon Rising*. New York: Scholastic, 2001. Garmon's book is part of the Universal Monsters series, in which three teens accidentally let six monsters loose in their small Florida town. In this story, the teens, Nina, Joe, and Bob, are trying to recapture the dreaded wolf man. Reports of attacks by a giant wolf set the trio on the right trail. But they soon find out that the wolf man has bitten someone and created another werewolf. Can Nina, Joe, and Bob stop the wolf man before he spreads his curse any further?

Philbrick, Rodman, and Lynn Hartnett. *Night Creatures*. New York: Scholastic, 1996. The first book in the Werewolf Chronicles, *Night Creatures* tells the story of Gruff, a human boy abandoned as a toddler in the woods. Gruff is found and adopted by a wolf family, and he lives with them happily for many years. But one night, during a full moon, Gruff discovers that he's a werewolf. After he is "rescued" by people and brought to a nearby town, Gruff must fight against his werewolf impulses.

Wolf Song of Alaska
http://www.wolfsongalaska.org/
Wolf Song of Alaska is a nonprofit association dedicated to educational programs about wolves throughout the world. It also includes a section on "Wolves and Folklore" that looks at the many stories and images arising from interaction between humans and wolves. The section looks in particular at werewolf folklore and lycanthropy.

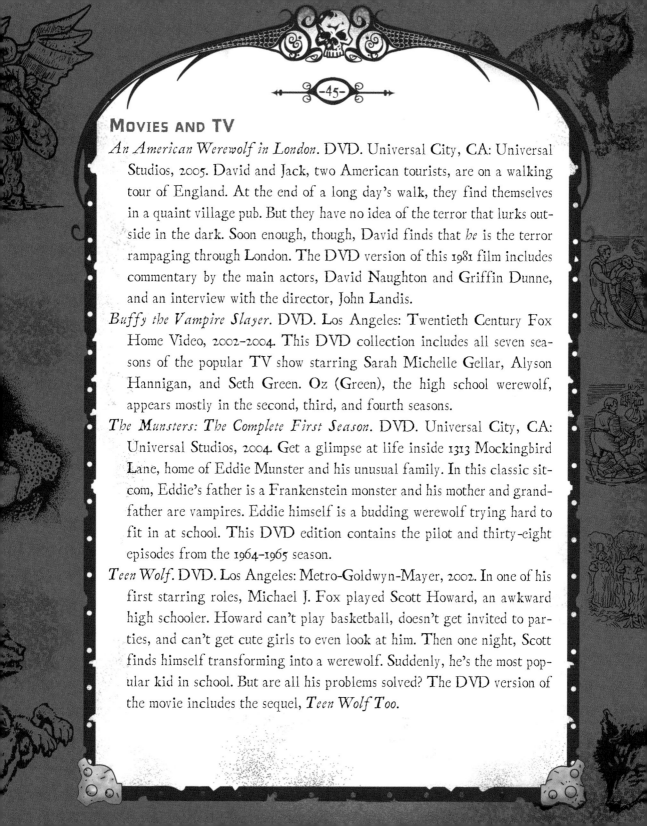

Movies and TV

An American Werewolf in London. DVD. Universal City, CA: Universal Studios, 2005. David and Jack, two American tourists, are on a walking tour of England. At the end of a long day's walk, they find themselves in a quaint village pub. But they have no idea of the terror that lurks outside in the dark. Soon enough, though, David finds that *he* is the terror rampaging through London. The DVD version of this 1981 film includes commentary by the main actors, David Naughton and Griffin Dunne, and an interview with the director, John Landis.

Buffy the Vampire Slayer. DVD. Los Angeles: Twentieth Century Fox Home Video, 2002–2004. This DVD collection includes all seven seasons of the popular TV show starring Sarah Michelle Gellar, Alyson Hannigan, and Seth Green. Oz (Green), the high school werewolf, appears mostly in the second, third, and fourth seasons.

The Munsters: The Complete First Season. DVD. Universal City, CA: Universal Studios, 2004. Get a glimpse at life inside 1313 Mockingbird Lane, home of Eddie Munster and his unusual family. In this classic sitcom, Eddie's father is a Frankenstein monster and his mother and grandfather are vampires. Eddie himself is a budding werewolf trying hard to fit in at school. This DVD edition contains the pilot and thirty-eight episodes from the 1964–1965 season.

Teen Wolf. DVD. Los Angeles: Metro-Goldwyn-Mayer, 2002. In one of his first starring roles, Michael J. Fox played Scott Howard, an awkward high schooler. Howard can't play basketball, doesn't get invited to parties, and can't get cute girls to even look at him. Then one night, Scott finds himself transforming into a werewolf. Suddenly, he's the most popular kid in school. But are all his problems solved? The DVD version of the movie includes the sequel, *Teen Wolf Too*.

The Werewolf of London. DVD. Universal City, CA: Universal Studios, 2001. This 1935 horror classic tells the story of Henry Hull, a botanist from London, England. Hull travels to Tibet in search of a rare plant that only blooms in moonlight. While out in the field waiting for the bloom, Hull is bitten by a werewolf. At home in London, he begins transforming at night. When Hull realizes that he is responsible for a rash of murders, he works feverishly on a cure for his cursed condition.

The Wolf Man. DVD. Los Angeles: Universal Studios, 2001. Much of what we know of wolf man lore comes to us from this classic 1941 movie. The film follows the story of Larry Talbot (Lon Chaney Jr.), an American who visits his father's English estate. While there, Talbot meets a gypsy fortune-teller. She warns him that anyone can become a werewolf if the circumstances are right. But Talbot has no time for the gypsy's silly superstitions. Then one night, he is attacked by what he thinks is a wolf. At the next full moon, Talbot begins a terrifying transformation. Back in human form, he finds himself accused of murder. The DVD edition includes a commentary by film historian Tom Weaver and the documentary *Monster by Moonlight*.

INDEX

ABOUT THE AUTHOR

Stephen Krensky is the author of many fiction and nonfiction books for children, including titles in the On My Own Folklore series and *Vampires, Frankenstein, Dragons, The Mummy,* and *Bigfoot.* When he isn't hunched over his computer, he makes school visits and teaches writing workshops. In his free time, he enjoys playing tennis and softball and reading books by other people. Krensky lives in Massachusetts with his wife, Joan, and their family.

PHOTO ACKS

The images in this book are used with permission of: © Mary Evans Picture Library, pp. 2-3, 20; © Daniel J. Cox/CORBIS, p. 8; © Archivo Iconografico, S.A./CORBIS, p. 9; © Mary Evans Picture Library/Edwin Wallace, p. 10; © Historical Picture Archive/CORBIS, p. 12; © Raintree 1997/www.DogStampsPlus.com, p. 13; Fortean Picture Library, pp. 16, 25, 26, 28; © Duhamel Francois/CORBIS SYGMA, p. 17; © Bettmann/CORBIS, pp. 32, 33; © Underwood & Underwood/CORBIS, p. 34; © Swim Ink 2, LLC/CORBIS, p. 35; © The Granger Collection, New York, p. 36; © Neal Preston/CORBIS, p. 37; © Wolfkill/The Kobal Collection, p. 38; © CBS Photo Archive/Getty Images, p. 39; © Polygram/Universal/The Kobal Collection, p. 40. Illustrations by Bill Hauser, pp. 1, 6-7, 14-15, 19, 22-23, 29, 30-31. All page backgrounds illustrated by Bill Hauser.

Front Cover: © Photofest